THE MUSLIM WORLD

Richard Tames

MACDONALD

Editor
Frances Merrett
Design
Roland Blunk
Picture Research
Jenny Golden
Production
Rosemary Bishop

The author and publishers are very grateful
to Dr. M. A. S. Abdel-Haleem of the School
of Oriental and African Studies (University
of London) for his advice in the preparation
of this book.

First published 1982
Reprinted 1984
Macdonald & Co. (Publishers) Ltd.,
Maxwell House, Worship Street
London EC2A 2EN
A Member of BPCC plc

ISBN 0 356 07520 6

Made and printed by
Henri Proost, Turnhout, Belgium

Cover picture: The Mahabet Khan mosque
at Peshawar, Pakistan.

Endpapers: Calligraphic tilework from the
Rustum Pasha Mosque in Istanbul, Turkey.

Title page: Mecca at night.

Contents page: Reading the Qur'an in the
mosque, Jiblah.

Contents

Who are the Muslims?

Right Many people think of Muslims as being Arabs. In fact Arabs make up only about one-sixth of the world's Muslim population.

Right Wherever Muslims live, and whatever their language, they all observe the same basic rituals of prayer in Arabic, as here in Nigeria.

Right The Muslim world is undergoing profound and rapid changes, symbolized by the contrasting dress of different generations in this Turkish family gathered outside a mosque in Istanbul, Turkey.

God's will

Islam is an Arabic word which means 'submitting'. Islam is the religion based on the will of God as revealed to humanity by Prophets sent since the beginning of time. A follower of this religion is a Muslim, a person who is submitting to God's will and trying to live in the way that they believe God requires them to.

Worldwide following

There are Muslims in almost every country in the world. In more than fifty countries Muslims form the majority of believers. Most of these Muslims live in the great belt of arid lands stretching from Morocco to Pakistan; others live in West Africa and South East Asia.

Indonesia, followed by Bangladesh and Pakistan have the largest Muslim populations but there are also tens of millions living as minorities in India, China and the USSR. Other minorities are to be found in East Africa, the West Indies, Yugoslavia and Western Europe.

Many of the Muslims living in Western Europe (such as the Turks in West Germany and the North African Arabs in France) have come to work there rather than to settle.

Britain's Muslim population is very mixed, consisting of students from Nigeria and Malaysia, businessmen from the Middle East and East Africa and former farmers from Pakistan, Bangladesh and India. Many of these people now regard Britain as their

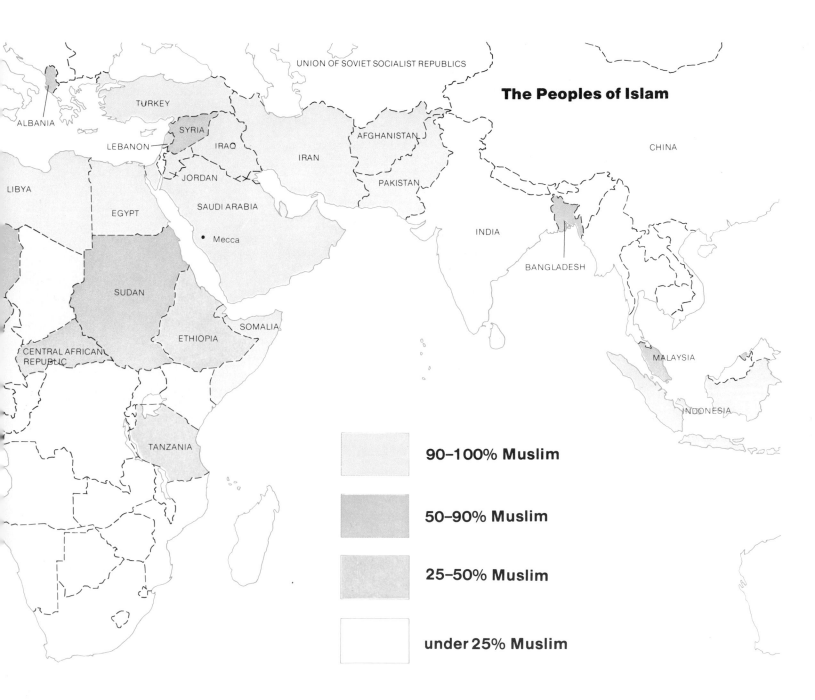

The Peoples of Islam

UNION OF SOVIET SOCIALIST REPUBLICS

ALBANIA

TURKEY

LEBANON
SYRIA
IRAQ
JORDAN
IRAN
AFGHANISTAN
PAKISTAN

CHINA

LIBYA

EGYPT

SAUDI ARABIA

• Mecca

INDIA

BANGLADESH

SUDAN

SOMALIA

ETHIOPIA

CENTRAL AFRICAN
REPUBLIC

MALAYSIA

INDONESIA

TANZANIA

90–100% Muslim

50–90% Muslim

25–50% Muslim

under 25% Muslim

Above Mecca, in Saudi Arabia, lies at the heart of the Muslim world.

permanent home where they look for education and a good future for their families.

United by the Qur'an and Five Pillars
Muslims are united by their belief in the Qur'an (Koran: the holy book of Islam) and their wish to follow the example of Muhammad, its Prophet, even though they live in so many countries, speak different languages and follow different customs in daily life. They also accept the same five duties as 'pillars of the faith'. These are:
Shahadah —to confess their belief—'I

witness that there is no god but Allah and that Muhammad is the Prophet of Allah.'
(Allah is an Arabic word meaning 'the God'.)
Salat —to pray five times a day.
Zakat —to give alms for the needy.
Saum —to fast in the month of Ramadan.
Hajj —to make the pilgrimage to Mecca.
   Islam also means 'peace'. Muslims greet each other by saying '*as-salaamu alaykum*' (peace be upon you). They believe that when all people submit to Allah's will and live by the Qur'an, peace will come to everyone.

The story of Muhammad

Mecca—Muhammad's birthplace

Muhammad was born in the trading city of Mecca, in about the year 570 of the Christian era. His early life was passed in poverty because both his parents had died by the time he was six years old. Later on while working as a trader Muhammad soon became known as *al-Amin* (the trustworthy). When he was 25 he married his employer, a rich widow of 40 called Khadijah.

He could have had an easy life. But he was troubled by conditions in Mecca. The rich merchants oppressed the poor. There was much gambling, drunkenness and violence. Women and children were often cruelly treated. Although the city had a famous shrine, the Ka'aba, the religion of the day seemed cruel and useless. The people believed in many gods and worshipped idols. Muhammad thought that making sacrifices to idols was senseless. He retired for long periods to the mountains around Mecca to meditate.

God's message

Muhammad was sitting in a cave on Mount Hira, when he sensed the presence of a strange being. This was perceived by him as the angel Gabriel, who commanded Muhammad in the following words:

'Recite! In the Name of thy Lord who created, created Man from congealed blood.' This was Muhammad's first revelation from God, which is the first part of the Qur'an.

Muhammad told the Meccans (people of Mecca) that there was only one God, *Allah*, (*the* God) and that the worship of idols was wicked. He said that God was the Creator of the world and there would be a day of Judgement when every man and woman would be sent to Heaven or Hell. Some of the Meccans became his followers but many of the most powerful people turned against him and said that he was either lying or mad. Many of Muhammad's followers were beaten and insulted.

The departure

At last, in 622, Muhammad accepted an invitation from the people of Medina to go and live among them. He and his followers left Mecca. This event is known as the *hijra* (the departure). It marks the beginning of the Muslim calendar because, at Medina, Muhammad established the first Muslim community.

Above The Prophet's Mosque in Medina. Muhammad's tomb lies beneath the green dome.

Pre-Islamic Trade Routes

Mediterranean

PERSIA

EGYPT

Mecca

ARABIA

Red Sea

Arabian Sea

- - - ▶ Sea Routes
- - - ▶ Land Routes

Right Mecca during the lifetime of the Prophet was connected to many other countries by sea and land trade-routes.

The return to Mecca

While they were at Medina, raids and battles took place between the Muslims and the people of Mecca. At last, in 630 the Meccans were defeated and Muhammad returned in triumph to Mecca. The people accepted Islam as their religion and the idols were taken from the Ka'aba and destroyed.

In 632 Muhammad died. Abu Bakr, his close friend, told the people 'If there are any among you who worshipped Muhammad, he is dead. But if it is God you worship, He lives forever.'

'The prophets leave knowledge as their inheritance. The learned ones inherit this great fortune.'

saying of the Prophet Muhammad

11

How Islam spread

Right A century after the death of Muhammad the Muslims ruled an area stretching from the borders of India to Spain. Apart from Spain, the areas shown in green are still Muslim today.

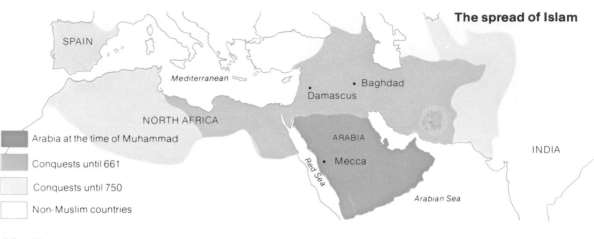

The spread of Islam

- Arabia at the time of Muhammad
- Conquests until 661
- Conquests until 750
- Non-Muslim countries

SPAIN · Mediterranean · NORTH AFRICA · Baghdad · Damascus · ARABIA · Mecca · Red Sea · Arabian Sea · INDIA

Right The Court of the Myrtles, at the Palace of the Alhambra, at Granada in southern Spain. The Spanish language and Spanish architecture still bear many traces of the seven centuries of Moorish rule.

Muslim rule expands

After Muhammad's death some of the tribes who had become Muslims decided to give up Islam because they did not want to pay *zakat*. The Muslims chose Abu Bakr to be Caliph (*Khalifa* means successor).

He went to war against the tribes who had deserted Islam until they submitted. After the Muslims had conquered all Arabia they turned against the non-Muslim empires of Byzantium and Persia. Within a century a vast area was under Muslim rule.

The Muslims allowed the Christians and Jews in these lands to keep their religions but made them pay extra taxes.

Shiites and Sunni

Abu Bakr was followed as Caliph by other close companions of the Prophet—Umar and Uthman. In 656 Ali (Muhammad's cousin and son-in-law) became Caliph but he was murdered in 661 and was succeeded by a member of the Umayyad family. Ali's supporters, the *Shi'at-Ali* (party of Ali) carried on fighting for his son Hussein, who was killed in 680.

The descendants of these people became known as the Shia or Shiites. They are a minority group in Islam and have some beliefs and customs which differ from the majority, called Sunni, who follow the *Sunna* (tradition) of the Prophet. Nowadays the Shia form the majority of the population in Iraq and Iran.

Baghdad—the new capital

The Umayyad dynasty was overthrown in 750 by descendants of the Prophet's uncle, Abbas. The Abbasids moved the capital of the empire from Damascus to the new city of Baghdad. When Baghdad was destroyed by the Mongols in 1258 the Abbasids' rule ended.

By then the empire had for some time ceased to be one territory ruled from a single centre. Local princes and generals tried to make themselves independent wherever they could. At one time there were three rulers claiming to be Caliph. But as a civilization Islam remained united by the Arabic language, by laws based on the Qur'an and by ties of trade and pilgrimage.

Below The Dome of the Rock in Jerusalem, third holiest city of Islam, is the first great Muslim building. Built at the end of the 7th century, it was restored in the 16th century by the Ottoman architect Sinan. Muslims believe that the rock sheltered by this mosque is the spot from which the call to judgement will be sounded on the last day.

Islamic empires

Right In the 16th and 17th centuries the Ottoman, Safavid and Mughal empires dazzled Europeans with their power and splendour.

The greatest extent of the major Islamic Empires

Vienna

Istanbul

Mediterranean Sea

Isfahan • PERSIA

EGYPT

ARABIA

AFRICA

Delhi
Fatehpur Sikri • • Agra

INDIA

Indian Ocean

■ Ottoman

□ Safavid

■ Mughal

The Ottoman Empire

Of the three great Muslim empires which had been founded by the mid-16th century the Ottoman Empire was the one which lasted the longest. It began with the 13th-century conquests of Osman, a Turkish nomad chief. Osman's descendants crushed the Byzantine Empire and after 1453 made its capital (Constantinople) their own, but re-named it Istanbul. The court of Suleyman II so dazzled European visitors that they called him 'the Magnificent'.

Right The Shah's Mosque, Isfahan, is still the glory of this purpose-built capital.

The Ottomans twice laid siege to Vienna but the climate and great distances involved set limits on their powers of conquest. In 1699 the Ottomans signed a treaty giving up territory for the first time but it was only defeat in the First World War (1914–18) that finally brought the empire to an end.

The Safavid Empire

The Ottomans fought many border wars against the Safavid rulers of Persia, whose main achievement was to make Shiite Islam the official religion of their country. Under Shah Abbas a magnificent new capital was built at Isfahan. In the 18th century the Safavids were followed by the weak Qajar dynasty.

The Mughal Empire

Safavid Persia also fought against its other neighbour, the Mughal Empire. The Mughal Empire was founded by Babur, almost lost by his son Humayun but regained by Akbar (Babur's grandson) who doubled the size of its territory.

Akbar reigned at almost exactly the same time as Queen Elizabeth I of England. Like her he was a great patron of the arts and lavishly praised by courtiers. He built massive palace forts at Delhi and Agra as well as a whole new capital at Fatehpur Sikri which was abandoned almost as soon as it was completed.

In 1739 the Persians sacked Delhi and carried off a fabulous, jewelled Peacock throne. The Mughal Empire never really recovered and its power passed gradually into the hands of the British, who stayed as rulers until 1947.

Common features

These three Islamic empires—Ottoman, Safavid and Mughal—had a number of features in common. The ruling class was not Arab in those empires. The Ottomans relied on Christian converts, recruited as boys, to serve as civil servants and members of the famed Janissary corps of troops. In each empire the power of gunpowder was used to make remote provinces obey the power of central government. Each court was a place of splendour, luxury and intrigue. Each, at its height, was more powerful than any comparable state in Europe.

15

The Qur'an

Right Because Muslims believe the Qur'an (Koran) to be the literal word of God they have always been prepared to lavish much time and skill on making it look splendid and impressive.

Making a beautiful Qur'an has long been regarded as a pious act and the finest calligraphers using the best materials were employed to record God's word for the benefit of humanity.

The actual word of God

Muslims believe that the Qur'an is the actual word of God. Muhammad was not, therefore, the 'author' of the Qur'an. Muslims believe that Muhammad was the man through whom God chose to speak to mankind. The word *Qur'an* in Arabic means 'recitation'. The first lines revealed to the Prophet begin with the command 'Recite'.

During the lifetime of the Prophet various parts of the Qur'an were written down. A number of the early Muslims learned them by heart. After the Prophet's death a final version of the Qur'an was put together, and Muslims believe that this represents God's last and complete message to mankind.

The Qur'an is arranged in 114 suras (chapters), each of which has a name. These do not occur in the order in which they were revealed to the Prophet. Scholars generally regard Sura 96 (The Congealed Blood) as the one that was first revealed to Muhammad. The first sura *Al-Fatihah* (The Opening) is recited in each of the daily prayers. Apart from this one, the other suras are organized in the approximate order of their length, with the longer suras coming at the beginning and the shorter ones at the end. This roughly reverses the order in which they came to the Prophet. The shorter suras, revealed while he was still at Mecca, tell of God and Judgement and Heaven and Hell.

Rules for living

The longer suras, revealed when he was leading the Muslim community at Medina, contain more detailed rules about how Muslims should live.

Muslims believe that because the Qur'an is God's final revelation to mankind it is perfect. They believe that the holy books of the Christians and the Jews, the Gospels and the Torah, are to be respected but that they do not contain the truth of God's message intact.

Because Muslims believe that the Qur'an is God's actual and final word they regard it as the most important book in the world. Traditional education in Muslim countries has always been based on a most detailed study of the Qur'an. Many scholars learn it completely by heart.

No translation except for study

Muslims also believe that the Qur'an, which was revealed in Arabic, cannot be translated adequately. Any translation misses something of its meaning. Therefore Muslims always learn it in Arabic, though for many of them it is not the language they usually speak. Translations may be used for the purpose of study.

The Qur'an is composed in a style which is half-prose and half-poetry. It has a very strong rhythm which has a powerful effect on Muslims who hear it read aloud. When Muhammad began to proclaim his revelations many of the unbelievers in Mecca called on him to perform miracles to prove that he was a prophet. Muhammad replied that he was an ordinary man and not divine. His only miracle was the Qur'an itself. The people who heard it had to admit that it was language of the greatest power and beauty.

Muslims believe that this power and beauty is proof of the Qur'an's divine origin. Ever since Muhammad, the Qur'an has been regarded as the most perfect use of the Arabic language.

Because Muslims regard the Qur'an as God's word they treat copies of it with the greatest respect. It is usually kept wrapped up and placed on a shelf for safety. While it is being read aloud Muslims will sit quietly, listening with complete attention.

'The best of you is he who has learnt the Qur'an and then taught it.'

'None of you has faith unless I am dearer to him than his father, and his son and all mankind.'

sayings of the Prophet Muhammad

Right The Qur'an has always been the foundation of education throughout the Muslim world. Believers are encouraged to learn by heart as much of it as they can.

The Five Pillars

Belief and action

Ask any Muslim to explain Islam and it is quite likely that he or she will talk about the 'five pillars of the faith'. It is important to note that these are matters of action as well as belief. They involve the individual believer in acting with others as a member of a world-wide religious community.

The first pillar

The first pillar is the profession of faith (*shahadah*)—'*I witness that there is no god but Allah and that Muhammad is the Prophet of Allah.*' Anyone who makes this statement publicly and sincerely can become a Muslim by that simple act.

Muslims believe that Allah 'the Merciful, the Compassionate' made the world, is all-powerful and all-seeing. He will judge all men and women at the end of time, sending them to Hell or Heaven according to their deeds. Muslims revere Jesus as a Prophet among many other Prophets such as Moses and Abraham but do not believe that he was divine. This is the main difference of belief that separates them from Christians.

Right Muslims see in the fruitfulness and beauty of a garden clear proof of God as the Creator of the World.

Right Each of the five daily prayers consists of a set cycle of ritual movements and prayers in Arabic which denote the believers' willing submission to God.

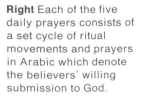

Positions of prayer

The second pillar

The second pillar is prayer five times a day (*salat*). Before praying a Muslim must wash his face, arms, head and feet. The prayers are said in Arabic and follow a fixed series of words and movements.

Prayers may be said in any clean place but adult male Muslims should go to the mosque for the noon prayer on Fridays. Prayer serves as a constant reminder of God's teachings to mankind and man's duty to praise and obey Him.

The third pillar

The third pillar of the faith is *zakat*, the act of giving each year a set proportion of one's wealth to help the needy and to support such good causes as building mosques or providing scholarships for students.

The fourth and fifth pillars

The fourth and fifth pillars are fasting in the month of Ramadan (*saum*) (see pp 22–23) and making the pilgrimage to Mecca (*hajj*) (see pp 24–25). Muslims are also obliged by their faith to be honest, just and generous and to be ready to fight in its defence. They are also forbidden to eat pork, to drink alcohol, to gamble or to lend money for interest.

Muslims believe that these rules are based on God's commands and cannot be altered. They provide a framework for a healthy society in which the religion, wealth and honour of all are made safe and secure.

'*Worship Allah as if you see Him; if you do not see Him, know that He sees you.*'

saying of the Prophet Muhammad

Right Prayers may be offered in any clean place, even in the street.

Mosques

Right The Islamic Cultural Centre on the edge of Regent's Park in London is the site of a splendid new mosque.

Simple beginnings

The first mosque was built in Medina by the Prophet and his closest followers. It was a very simple building with a roof of palm fronds held up by tree trunks. Many mosques of the early conquest years were converted Christian churches. Others, like the great mosque at Kairouan, in Tunisia, were built from stones and pillars taken from Roman ruins. Gradually Muslim architects began to design splendid buildings such as the Dome of the Rock mosque in Jerusalem and the Ibn Tulun mosque in Cairo.

Similar basic design

Mosques vary greatly in detail. In West Africa they are normally built of mud, in Iran they are often surfaced with tiles, but most have the same general features. There is an open courtyard with a water supply, where worshippers can gather and wash before going into the covered area of the prayer-hall. This is often divided into two parts to separate men and women. There are no pews because Muslims need the floor to pray on.

Muslims always pray facing towards Mecca so it is important for them to know the *qibla* (the direction of prayer). The qibla wall therefore contains an empty arch, the *mihrab*, which indicates the direction of Mecca. Next to the mihrab there is often a *minbar*, a pulpit with steps, from which the sermon is given at the noon prayer on Friday. Large mosques have an official *imam* (prayer leader) to give the sermon and lead the prayers but any adult male Muslim can lead the prayers if necessary.

Minaret

Riwaqs shady arcades

The call to prayer

The most noticeable external feature of the mosque is the minaret, a tall tower from which the muezzin calls the people to prayer with these words:

God is most great, God is most great, God is most great, God is most great, I bear witness that there is no god but Allah, I bear witness that there is no god but Allah, I bear witness that Muhammad is the messenger of Allah, I bear witness that Muhammad is the messenger of Allah. Come to prayer, Come to prayer. Come to your good, Come to your good. God is most great, God is most great. There is no god but Allah.

Apart from prayer the mosque is also used as a place for teaching, for meetings and for quiet meditation.

Right The National Mosque at Kuala Lumpur, Malaysia, was opened in 1964 and has room for 8,000 worshippers.

Below Simplicity and grandeur are the hallmarks of mosque architecture. Details may vary greatly but the basic elements of a courtyard, a prayer-hall, facilities for ablution and usually a minaret, are always present in the larger mosques.

An Islamic Mosque

Fauwara ablutions fountain

Zulla prayer hall

Sahn courtyard

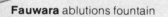

Mihrab alcove denoting direction of prayer

Minbar raised pulpit

Maqsura open-work screen

Qibla Wall indicates the direction of Mecca

Fasting and feasting

Right Congregational prayers, as seen here in the Cameroon, are an important part of both the Eid festivals.

Ramadan

Ramadan is the ninth month of the Muslim calendar and special because it was the month in which the Prophet first began to receive revelations from God. To remind them of this Muslims are supposed to fast for every one of the thirty days of Ramadan from dawn (when one can first tell a white thread from a black one) to sunset (when one can no longer do so). This means that they should not eat or drink anything at all, nor smoke, nor have sexual relations during this time.

Right After the Eid ul-Fitr prayers at the mosque, a London family enjoys a special snack before going out to visit relatives.

During this month they should also say extra prayers and try to read the whole of the Qur'an. They should be particularly careful not to quarrel with friends and neighbours but should try to be particularly kind and helpful.

Fasting

Fasting in Ramadan teaches Muslims to value the good things God has provided for their enjoyment and to remember the sufferings of the poor and the hungry. Fasting is held to develop self-discipline and an attitude of generosity toward others.

All adult Muslims must keep the fast but very old people, the sick and women who are pregnant or feeding a baby are excused. Travellers may eat while they are on a journey but must make up the lost days later on.

Festival of Eid ul-Fitr

At the end of Ramadan comes the festival of Eid ul-Fitr. Muslims put on their best clothes and go to the mosque to pray together. Elaborate meals are prepared and served and visits made to relatives and friends. Children are given sweets and presents and new clothes to mark this happy occasion.

Festival of Eid ul-Adha

The other main festival of Islam is Eid ul-Adha, the festival of sacrifice, which celebrates Abraham's willingness to sacrifice his son Ishmael on God's orders. Through this festival Muslims record their willingness to sacrifice what they hold dear in order to carry out God's commands.

Eid ul-Adha occurs in the month of Dhul-hijja and coincides with the pilgrimage to Mecca. It is celebrated on the anniversary of the day when the Qur'an, God's revelation through Muhammad, was finally declared complete. Eid ul-Adha is also marked by the wearing of one's best clothes and prayer at the mosque. Muslims who can afford to do so sacrifice an animal and share the meat with their friends and relatives and the poor.

In Muslim countries these two festivals are celebrated as public holidays and shops, offices and schools are closed. Other Muslim festivals include the anniversary of the birth of the Prophet, the death of Ali's son Hussein at the battle of Kerbala and the anniversary of the Hijra (the Muslim New Year).

Meat prepared in a special way

Muslims may only eat meat that has been killed in a particular way. This involves the use of a sharp knife which must penetrate the inner part of the animal's neck. When the animal is being slaughtered the butcher should say *Bismillah* (in the name of God) to show that life is being taken only to provide for man's need for food. The blood is then drained from the carcase. Meat prepared in this way is called *halal* (permitted) meat.

Forbidden items

Muslims are also forbidden to eat the meat of the pig in any form. This not only means pork, bacon and ham but also any product containing pig fat (lard), such as biscuits or ice cream. For this reason Muslims need to know the ingredients of any item they buy while shopping.

Alcohol in any form is absolutely forbidden to Muslims. They should not provide it for their non-Muslim guests and should not take profits from it by selling it.

Right A fair outside the Al-Aksa mosque in Jerusalem marks the celebration of Eid ul-Fitr by local Arab children.

A pilgrimage to Mecca

Right The hajj is a physical journey which becomes a spiritual experience as the pilgrim re-enacts significant incidents in the lives of the Prophets at the sites associated with them.

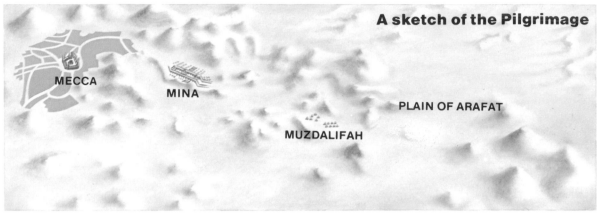

A sketch of the Pilgrimage

MECCA

MINA

MUZDALIFAH

PLAIN OF ARAFAT

Journey of a lifetime

Once in his or her lifetime a Muslim is obliged to undertake the *hajj* (the pilgrimage to Mecca). Only Muslims who can afford to do so are obliged to go. Muslims whose families would suffer by their absence should not go.

For most pilgrims their arrival in Arabia comes at the end of a long journey. They are reminded of the special purpose of their journey when they approach Mecca. Non-Muslims are forbidden to enter this area.

Simple dress

Male pilgrims wear only two seamless sheets of white cotton. This is because all of them, rich or poor, young or old, must look alike because they are alike in the sight of God. (There is no special costume for women but they must keep their faces unveiled.) During the pilgrimage the pilgrims are forbidden to use soap or perfumes, to have sexual relations, to cut their hair or nails, to kill any living thing or even to pick wild flowers.

Seven stages

Upon reaching Mecca the pilgrim walks seven times round the Ka'aba. He then runs seven times between the hills of Safa and Marwa. This commemorates the incident when Hagar, the mother of Ishmael (ancestor of the Arab people), searched in the desert for water for her son and God caused the holy well of Zem-Zem to gush forth nearby.

On the eighth day of the month of Dhul-Hijjah the pilgrim stays overnight at Mina and then on the ninth day goes to the plain of Arafat, where Muhammad preached his last sermon. Here all the pilgrims gather and pray until nightfall. After staying overnight at Muzdalifah the pilgrim goes back to Mina to perform the ritual of stoning the devils.

Right Buses, cars and umbrellas show how the products of the modern world have made the pilgrimage less arduous. Modern medicines also help to prevent the outbreak of epidemics.

Above Arafat, scene of the Prophet's last sermon, is visited by every Muslim who undertakes the pilgrimage to Mecca.

Seven stones are thrown at three stone pillars to commemorate Abraham's rejection of Satan.

Then the pilgrim sacrifices an animal and has his head shaved. After a final seven circuits of the Ka'aba the rites of pilgrimage are completed. Many pilgrims, however, go on to visit Medina, where the Prophet Muhammad is buried.

For fourteen centuries Muslims have undertaken the hajj. It is the world's largest annual spiritual gathering. Muslims from all over the world remember their unity by taking part in a common act of worship.

Daily life

Muslims in the developing world

Most Muslims live in the developing world. Perhaps because so many people think of them as Arab sheikhs (although five-sixths of all Muslims are not Arabs at all), they imagine them as nomads, living in the desert with herds of camels. Of course there are no deserts in the most populous Muslim countries, such as Indonesia and Bangladesh. And even in the Middle East Bedouin are only a tiny fraction of the population, perhaps 1%.

The cities of the developing world are growing rapidly. But the fact remains that the mass of the people in Muslim countries are villagers, working on the land or supplying people's daily needs through such crafts as carpentry, pottery and weaving. Families keep in close touch and relatives give each other help and advice.

Rural life

Villages in Muslim countries show the importance of Islam in the people's everyday life. The mosque is usually the largest building and often there is more than one. The idea that men and women should keep apart can be seen in the fact that only men go to the village guest-house or sit at the tables of the café, while women gather to talk at the well or in each other's houses.

Homes usually have strong doors and small windows and are built to face inwards onto a courtyard. Much of the household work is done in the courtyards and on the flat roofs. Family life is something to be kept private from outsiders. Visitors to a home will be shown into a guest-room and received by the men of the family, while the women stay in the background.

Muslims regard Islam as a complete way

Below The social life of women is essentially a private matter but Muslim men may gather freely in public, as is shown at this café in Oman.

of life which involves directly religious practices such as prayer and also covers aspects of daily life such as food and drink.

Wealth

The laws and customs of Islam also affect how wealth can be earned and how it should be spent. Many passages in the Qur'an condemn the misuse of wealth. The Qur'an also sets out detailed rules for the inheritance of property. A Muslim is forbidden to deprive his family of a share in his estate. Muslims are also forbidden to lend money for interest (usury) or to gamble.

Death

Because Muslims believe in the resurrection of the body after death, they are always buried, never cremated. Before burial the body is washed (unless the believer has died in battle) and wrapped in a shroud. Then a funeral prayer is said. It is a duty laid upon all Muslims to see that believers have a proper funeral.

Women do not usually attend the burial but often visit the grave for years afterwards.

'Charity is incumbent on each person every day. Charity is assisting anyone, lifting provisions, saying a good word; every step one takes walking to prayer is charity, showing the way is charity.'

'Say part of your prayers at home so your houses do not become like graves.'

'There are two blessings which most people misuse—health and leisure.'

sayings of the Prophet Muhammad

Below The flat roofs and enclosed courtyards of this Tunisian city provide areas for women to work and relax, and symbolize the emphasis in Islam on the privacy of family life.

Childhood

Right Circumcision is an important ceremony in the life of Muslim boys. In some countries this is performed a few days after birth, but in Turkey it is done when boys are 7, 9, 11 or 13 years old. Special clothes are worn for the occasion.

Learning about Islam from birth

When Muslims become parents they have a special responsibility to ensure that their children grow up understanding their faith and what it requires of them. The very first thing a Muslim baby hears on coming into the world is the *shahadah* (the profession of faith)—'*I witness that there is no god but Allah and that Muhammad is the Prophet of Allah.*'

Muslim boys are circumcised, usually while they are still very young. There is nothing in the Qur'an that requires this but it has always been the custom among Muslims. The circumcision of a boy is an occasion for feasting and celebration.

Observing parents

Muslim children first learn about their religious duties by watching their parents, for instance at prayer. As they get older they are shown how to pray, taught to memorize parts of the Qur'an and encouraged to begin keeping the fast of Ramadan, at first for a day at a time and then for longer periods. By the time they are twelve or thirteen years old they should be able to carry out their religious duties like an adult.

Reciting the Qur'an

Learning to read and recite the Qur'an has always been an important part of education in Muslim countries. Nowadays schools in many Muslim countries make this part of the regular curriculum. In others and in many non-Muslim countries, Muslim children go to special classes after school instead. These classes are often held in the mosque and taught by the local *imam* (leader of prayers in a mosque).

Respect for older relatives

As teenagers Muslims are expected to work hard at school and to help around the house. Going out alone to parties and discos is discouraged, especially for girls. On the whole girls tend to be treated more strictly than boys. Teenagers of both sexes, however, are expected to show great respect towards their older relatives and to enjoy the company of their family.

'*Be careful of your duty to Allah and be fair and just to your children.*'

saying of the Prophet Muhammad

Right These people are members of one family in Iran who live together in the same village. Muslim families in the West are often widely scattered but still keep in very close touch with one another.

Below Traditional education was based almost solely on the Qur'an. Nowadays, as at this school in Pakistan, children must study other subjects as well.

Marriage

Arranged marriages

In Islam a happy family life is regarded as the foundation of a healthy society. The Qur'an encourages Muslims to marry and have children. It also emphasizes that sexual relationships outside marriage are always wrong.

Marriages between Muslims are often arranged by the parents and older relatives of the people involved. The prospective bride and groom have the right to refuse the person chosen for them and the marriage cannot go ahead if both partners do not agree.

In practice most young Muslims seem to trust their parents to make a good choice for them. Muslims believe that because parents know all about their children they will look for partners whose upbringing and personality will enable the couple to get on well together and also fit in with the life of the family as a whole.

Among Muslims marriage is thought of as more than a matter for two individuals. It involves all of the many relatives and therefore family opinion is a very important factor in bringing about marriages and encouraging them to last.

Rarely more than one wife

Muslim men are allowed to marry up to four wives but it is (and always has been) very rare for most ordinary Muslims to have more than one wife. Islamic law requires that each wife be treated equally in every respect. Few husbands can afford to support two wives for economic reasons (let alone four), so polygamous marriages are very much the exception rather than the rule.

Muslims do however think that it is good to be able to take a second wife if the first is unable to have children or becomes so ill that she needs someone to look after her and the household.

A wife's first duty

Looking after the home and family is a Muslim wife's first duty. She is not expected to work outside the home to add to the family's income and indeed this is often frowned upon. Providing for the family is the main duty of the husband, though both parents bear responsibility for the upbringing of their children.

In most Muslim countries the family is a large group, consisting of many uncles and aunts and cousins, rather than the small parents-and-children group which is often thought of as the family in the West.

Members of this large, extended family network are expected to help each other in business matters or with domestic problems and to celebrate together at times of happiness. To be regarded as a fully adult member of this group a Muslim must really be married and have children of his or her own.

Divorce

Divorce is permitted in Islam but the Prophet said that it was the most hateful of all permitted things in the sight of God. Before Muslims get to the point of divorce they are encouraged to make every effort to reconcile their differences.

If divorce does occur the wife receives some money from her ex-husband and also takes all their household goods and furniture. But her maintenance then becomes the responsibility of her male relatives.

Right A Muslim bridegroom, veiled with flowers according to the custom of India and Pakistan, waits for his bride, accompanied by an imam.

Right A Bedouin wedding. The binding part of the ceremony is the signing and witnessing of a contract of marriage. The bride need not actually be present.

Women in Islam

Different duties

In Islam women and men have equal rights but different duties. Women have the same religious obligations as men, although they are excused attendance at the mosque on Fridays, so that they can be with their families.

Women have the same right as men to own property and to be educated, though in practice these rights have not always been respected by Muslim men. Islamic law also guarantees women a share in the property of their male relatives when they die, although they only receive half a man's portion of the inheritance. This is because Muslim men are bound to support their female relatives but Muslim women are not obliged to support their male relatives.

Caring for the family

Islam expects that men will chiefly be concerned with work and public affairs. The home and the care of the family are the main business of women. Indeed, one of the most famous of the Prophet's sayings was that paradise is to be found at the feet of your mother.

Working outside the home

Muslim women are allowed to work outside the home, providing this does not prevent them from taking proper care of their domestic duties. The sort of jobs that are favoured for Muslim women are caring occupations like nursing or teaching.

Women also do a vast amount of the agricultural work in villages and play a leading part in craft industries, especially textiles. Farm-work and carpet-weaving can, however, usually be done at or near home and do not usually involve going away or working with strangers.

Guidelines for dress

The Qur'an requires men and women to behave modestly and decently towards one another. The Islamic ideal of modest behaviour sets out certain general guidelines for how men and women should dress, but allows some variations to take account of different climates and customs.

Men should always be covered from the navel to the knees, even when swimming or taking a shower. They should not wear pure silk or gold or the special clothes associated

Right Women in Iran and other Muslim countries often reject Western dress in favour of traditional clothes.

Right Employment in the 'caring professions' is favoured for Muslim women. Here is Fawzia al-Sayegh, one of Kuwait's first women doctors, with a young patient.

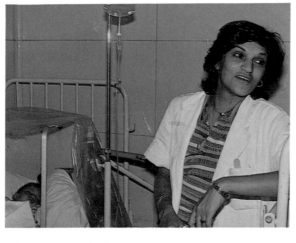

with other religions.

Women should cover their whole bodies except their faces and hands. Dresses should be loose and not reveal the shape of the body. Materials should not be transparent. When women are alone with close members of their family these rules need not be applied so strictly.

Great contrasts

The conditions of women's lives vary very greatly in different parts of the Muslim world, although everywhere they are changing because of Western influence, the growth of educational opportunities and the availability of birth-control. At present striking contrasts can be seen. In Syria and Iraq women are encouraged to work and take part in politics. In Saudi Arabia they are still not allowed to drive cars. The idea that women should live in *purdah* (seclusion), kept apart from men (except their male relatives) is still held to be important in many parts of the Muslim world.

The existence of the extended family means that women in purdah live not in isolation from one another but rather in their own women's world. However Muslim women who live in individual seclusion in non-Muslim countries far away from their relatives can often feel extremely isolated.

'Modesty is part of faith.'

'Visit the sick, feed the hungry and free the captives.'

'No one eats better food than that which he eats from the work of his own hands.'

sayings of the Prophet Muhammad

Right In Indonesia and West Africa women often run market stalls but in the Middle East it is usual for the men to do this and often the shopping as well.

Sufis

Right Sufi brotherhoods are headed by 'Shaykhs' who admit new disciples and supervise their training. Muslims who are not Sufis may also look to shaykhs for guidance in religious matters.

Right Many Sufis expressed their longing for God through poetry. The tomb of the Sufi poet Hafiz at Shiraz in Iran is set in a beautiful garden, a symbol of the Qur'anic vision of paradise.

Closer to God

Since the early days of Islam there have been Muslims who tried to become as close as possible to God. They were not content simply to follow the rules laid down in the Qur'an. Many of them believed that it contained secret meanings which could only be understood by long study or thought.

Other Muslims tried to leave the everyday world far behind by going without food or sleep. These Muslims came to be called Sufis because they wore a rough woollen robe (*suf*) to show that they were not interested in wealth or comfort. Over the years different brotherhoods of Sufis started, each following the examples and teachings of a famous Sufi master of the past.

Each Sufi brotherhood had its own special methods of reaching out towards God. Usually these methods were kept secret by members of the brotherhood who called them the *tariqa* (path). Some Sufis chant, some breathe rhythmically and others dance. Perhaps the most famous are the Mevlevi dervishes (now to be found in Turkey) who whirl round and round.

The search

What the Sufis are searching for cannot easily be explained. Some have tried to explain it through poetry. Others, although they have not been interested in riches and power, have been greatly respected as wise and holy men.

Learned Muslims have sometimes opposed the influence of Sufis over other Muslims and have disapproved of such customs as praying at the tombs of Sufi holy men. But the influence of Sufis in North and West Africa, Pakistan and India remains strong.

Al-Ghazali

One of the most famous of all Sufis was Al-Ghazali (d.1111). He was a great scholar who became a brilliant teacher. Students travelled hundreds of miles to hear his lectures in Baghdad. One day he decided that learning from books was not enough to give him a full knowledge of God. So he became a Sufi for many years. But he always insisted that the mystic also needed to have a sound grasp of the Qur'an and the traditions of the Prophet—otherwise he might just become the victim of his own imagination.

Examples of Sufi writing

إلهى إنْ كنتُ عبدتك من خوف النار فأحرقنى فى النار،
أو طمعاً فى الجنة فحرمها على، وإن كنت لا أعبدك
إلّا من أجلك فلا تحرمنى مشاهدة وجهك.

O my Lord, if I worship Thee from fear of Hell, burn me in Hell, and if I worship Thee from hope of Paradise, exclude me thence, but if I worship Thee for Thine own sake then withhold not from me Thine Eternal Beauty.

فليتك تحلو والحياة مريرة   وليتك ترضى والأنام غضب

وليت الذى بينى وبينك عامر   وبينى وبين العالمين خراب

إذا صح منك الود فالكل هيّن   وكل الذى فوق التراب تراب

Would that you are sweet to me even if life is bitter, pleased with me even if all else is angry.
Would that what is between you and me is flourishing even if what is between me and all else is desolate.
If I secure your love, then all else is insignificant and all on earth is nought but earth.

Rabia Al-Adawiyya, a Sufi woman poet who died in Iraq, 801

35

Islamic art

Right This fireplace, in the Topkapi Palace, Istanbul, well illustrates the skill of Muslim craftsmen in ceramics and metalwork. It also shows the use of floral and calligraphic motifs.

Far right The Alhambra palace in Granada is one of the few surviving glories of seven centuries of Muslim rule in Spain. Its cool gardens, complex tile and mosaic decoration and delicately carved stucco work have inspired Western as well as Muslim artists and architects.

No human or animal figures

Islam has created its own styles of art and architecture. Because Muhammad preached against the worship of idols, Muslim artists were discouraged from making paintings or sculptures of people or animals. Instead they used designs based on flowers and plants or geometric patterns, like stars.

Calligraphy as decoration

Calligraphy, the art of beautiful writing, was especially praised and rewarded because it was a way of reminding Muslims of God's words in the Qur'an. Quotations from the Qur'an and the sayings of the Prophet, as well as proverbs and poetry, were used to decorate buildings, tiles, pottery, metalware and textiles. This tradition also shows the continuing power and importance of the Arabs' delight in their language.

Right Although painting never acquired the same importance in Islam as in Western art, the illustration of books of poetry allowed scope for Muslim artists to use their skills.

Far right Elaborate jewellery has been worn by Muslim women for centuries not only as personal adornment but also as a way of displaying the wealth and prestige of their families.

Textiles as art

Textiles became especially important in Islamic art because wood was scarce in the Middle East so that woven items such as rugs, cushions and bags often took the place of beds, chairs and chests. They were particularly important to nomads, who could not carry much heavy furniture when they moved from place to place.

Beautiful gardens

Another form of art favoured by Muslim rulers was the creation of beautiful gardens. In the Qur'an paradise is often described as a garden. (The English word 'paradise' comes from a Persian word meaning 'garden'.) Cool, shady gardens with flowers and shrubs, pools and fountains were especially precious in the arid lands of the Middle East where Islam first spread.

Europeans learned many techniques, such as the use of pointed arches in buildings, from Muslim craftsmen. Pottery and carpets made by Muslim artists have been traded (and valued very highly) for centuries in non-Muslim countries all over the world.

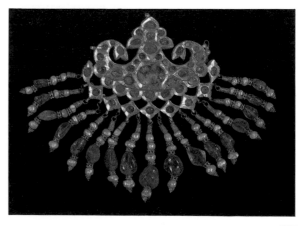

Scientific wonders

A search for knowledge

One of the most famous of the sayings of Muhammad was *'Look for knowledge, even as far away as China.'* Muslim rulers therefore encouraged scientists as well as artists. At Baghdad the Abbasids established a 'House of Wisdom' which was a great library and a translation centre where the writings of the ancient Greeks, Indians and Persians were translated into Arabic.

It is through these Arabic versions that European scholars first learned much of the scientific knowledge of the ancient world. Many modern English scientific terms (such as 'chemistry', 'zero' and 'rocket') come from Arabic. What are usually called Arabic numerals (1, 2, 3 and so on) were really invented in India, but it was Muslim scholars who worked out the full system of decimal calculation and passed it on to Europe, where it gradually replaced Roman numerals (I, II, III and so on).

Right A medieval treatise on the workings of the eye. Muslim scientists made important advances in optics and the treatment of eye diseases.

Right The need to find the direction of Mecca for the purposes of prayer gave Muslims an interest in astronomy from the earliest times. This astrolabe, made in the 17th century, was used to calculate the movements of stars and planets.

Far right This reconstruction of a pharmacy reminds us that traditional Muslim healers pioneered the use of many drugs and spread knowledge of their uses to the West. Many pharmacies sold a range of remedies and also made up prescriptions.

Drugs were carefully checked by inspectors who would call on a pharmacy at any time to make spot checks on the quality of drugs being sold. If a pharmacist was found to be cheating, the inspector could impose a heavy penalty such as a large fine or a beating.

Mathematics

Muslim scientists were especially interested in mathematics and astronomy. They practically invented algebra and trigonometry. These interests arose partly from the need to work out exactly the right times and direction for prayer. Muslims also had to plan their calendar and be able to work out how to share out inheritances according to the rules laid down in the Qur'an.

Medical research

In medicine Muslims concentrated on the use of drugs and herbs rather than surgery. They also knew about the importance of diet, climate and mental strain in affecting the health of patients. They became very expert in treating eye diseases which were very common in the Middle East. Muslims also set up public hospitals with trained, permanent staff, where young doctors could study and do research.

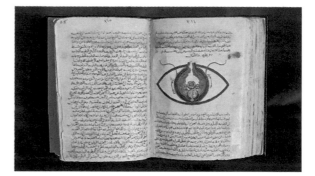

Amazing discoveries

Among the most famous Muslim scientists were Ibn al-Haytam (d.1039) who tried to find out how rainbows are caused, Ibn Sina (d.1037) who wrote a medical encyclopedia and described how epidemics spread, and al-Razi (d.925) who was the first scientist to tell the difference between smallpox and measles.

Astronomy and geography

Trade and pilgrimage encouraged Muslims to travel and in the deserts of the Middle East they often used the stars to help them find their way. Interest in astronomy and geography therefore had a practical value.

Al-Khwarizmi (d.846) was both a famous astronomer and a mathematician, as well as the compiler of the first Arabic atlas. Umar Khayyam (d.1123), who is better known in the West as a Sufi poet, was a court astronomer who devised a calendar as accurate as the one we use today.

Al-Biruni (d.1050) wrote a geography of India and guessed correctly that the Indus river valley must once have been a sea. Al-Idrisi (d.1166) compiled a famous atlas for Roger II, the Christian king of Italy.

'There is no disease for which Allah has not sent a cure.'

saying of the Prophet Muhammad

Modern Islam

Western colonization

Between the middle of the 18th century and the middle of the 20th century large parts of the Muslim world came under Western control. Many countries were conquered and ruled as colonies. Europeans at that time were entirely confident of the superiority of their technology, their military power, their religion, and indeed, their whole way of life.

One leader of a Muslim country even came to think that the Islamic way of life had made the people poor and backward. After the Ottoman Empire was defeated in the First World War the new leader of Turkey, Kemal Atatürk, brought in many changes in education and the laws. He even changed the calendar and the writing system and tried to make the people wear Western-style clothes. Most ordinary Turks, however, remained firm believers in traditional Muslim ways.

Achieving independence

Since the Second World War Muslim countries have regained their independence. As they have learned more about the West many Muslim leaders have come to believe that its way of life still has many problems and weaknesses, although most still admire its achievements in such fields as industry and medicine. Oil production and sales have given some influential Muslim countries (such as Saudi Arabia and Libya) great wealth. This has given them the opportunity to help poorer Muslim countries through foreign aid.

Far right Rising standards of education for women are widening opportunities for employment but, after marriage, the home and family should come first.

Right Even in modern Turkey traditional beliefs are a part of everyday life. This bumper-sticker calls on God's protection for a taxi-driver and his passengers.

Countries like Iran and Pakistan have turned against Western influences in recent years and called for a new commitment to Islamic ideals and ways. Even in countries where Western influences have been strong and long-established (as in Egypt and Tunisia) the trend towards strengthening Islamic traditions has also been seen.

In Malaysia students have organized bans on Western music and alcohol in the universities. These changes are not necessarily a threat to Western countries and their way of life but they do show that Muslims wish their customs and traditions to be treated equally. Muslims increasingly feel able to face the future with confidence and faith in the eternal message of Allah and the teachings of his Prophet, Muhammad.

In Europe, North America and the West Indies Muslims have become permanent members of the community, organizing their own mosques and charities and in some cases their own schools. Although they live in non-Muslim societies they wish to keep their character as Muslims, wherever they are.

'It is charity for any Muslim who plants a tree or cultivates land which provides food for a bird, animal or man.'

saying of the Prophet Muhammad

Right Television studios in Kuwait. The different parts of the Muslim world are now being drawn closer together by modern mass communications.

Right A conference of representatives of Muslim countries. Muslims are increasingly acting together in economic and educational matters as well as in politics.

Further Information

Useful words–a glossary

Adhan announcement—the call to prayer.

Ahl al-Kitab the people of the book—i.e. Jews and Christians, who possess books of revelation.

Allah God.

Ansar helpers—the first converts in Medina, later used to denote all those who helped the Prophet in his campaigns.

Bismallah abbreviation of '*bismillah al-rahman, al-rahim*'—'in the name of God, the merciful, the compassionate'. A standard invocation used by Muslims before any significant act, task or journey.

Dervish member of Sufi religious order.

Dhikr remembering, mentioning—recitation of the names of God is a central feature of Sufi ritual; each order has its distinctive dhikr.

Dhimmi 'people of the covenant'—Jews or Christians living under Muslim rule. These protected classes were allowed to practise their own religion in return for payment of a poll-tax but were forbidden to exercise full civil rights.

Eid ul-Adha see **Id al-Adha**.

Eid ul-Fitr see **Id al-Fitr**.

Hadith saying, statement—a record of something said or done by the Prophet.

Hajj the pilgrimage to Mecca.

Hajji a person who has performed the hajj.

Halal permitted.

Haram sacred—sanctuary, holy territory. Term used to denote the environs of Mecca, Medina and Jerusalem.

Hijra the Prophet's departure from Mecca to Medina; variously translated as flight, emigration, exodus and breaking of ties. The Islamic calendar dates from this era.

Ibadah worship (plural—*ibadet*).

Id al-Adha (Eid ul-Adha) feast of sacrifices. Major festival of the Muslim calendar, celebrated on the 10th Dhul-Hijja, the day on which pilgrims make their sacrifices in the valley of Mina.

Id al-Fitr (Eid ul-Fitr) feast of the breaking. Festival to mark the end of the fast of Ramadan.

Ihram state of ritual purity assumed by pilgrims about to undertake the rites of hajj.

Imam he who stands at the front, leader of prayers in a mosque.

Iman faith, belief.

Islam submitting (to God), peace.

Jihad struggle—term used to denote both war in defence of the faith and the effort to overcome one's imperfections to become a better Muslim.

Ka'aba cube—the central shrine of Islam in Mecca.

Kafir unbeliever.

Khalifa successor—(Caliph) title assumed by heads of the Muslim community after the death of the Prophet.

Kiswa black cloth covering the Ka'aba.

Khutba sermon delivered in mosque at congregational prayer on Fridays.

Masjid a place of prostration, a mosque.

Mihrab recess in mosque wall denoting the direction of prayer.

Minbar pulpit from which the khutba is delivered.

Mu'adhdhin person who gives the call to prayer (muezzin).

Muslim a follower of Islam.

Nabi prophet.

Qibla the direction of prayer.

Qur'an (Koran) recitation—the sacred book of Islam.

Rak'a complete cycle of prescribed ritual movements performed during prayer.

Ramadan ninth month of the Muslim calendar. A period of dawn-to-dusk fasting.

Salat a ritual prayer, observed five times a day.

Saum a fast.

Shahada the profession of faith—*La ilaha illa'llah, Muhammad rasul Allah*—there is no god but Allah (and) Muhammad is the Prophet of Allah.

Shia party, fashion—name for historic subdivision of the Muslim community. Members of the various Shia traditions differ with regard to details of doctrine and ritual.

Sufi an Islamic mystic.

Sunna custom, practice—the words and deeds of the Prophet.

Sura a chapter of the Qur'an.

Tawhid the Oneness of God.

Umma the community of Muslims.

Wudu ablution performed before prayer.

Zakat alms, tax.

The Muslim calendar

Islam has its own calendar, which dates from the *Hegira* (*Hijra*) when the Prophet and his companions left Mecca for Medina (16 July 622). The year 1400 AH (Anno Hegirae) began at sunset on 19 November 1979.

The Muslim calendar was inaugurated by the second Caliph, Umar, who was faced with the practical problems of administering a rapidly expanding empire in which correspondence over long distances had to be accurately dated.

The Qur'an (10:5) decrees the use of lunar months and the Islamic year is therefore out of phase with the Gregorian calendar, which is based on the solar year. The lunar year is roughly 11 days shorter than the solar year and its months have, by convention, 29 and 30 days alternately. In relation to the Western system of reckoning therefore, the Muslim calendar moves 'backward' each year. This means that Muslim festivals fall at different times of the Western year and bear no fixed relation to the seasons.

To calculate conversions from one calendar to the other

a) The rule of thumb is that a Western (i.e. Gregorian) century equals 103 years according to the Muslim calendar. (And the year 1300 corresponded with 700 AH.)

b) A more exact formula is that where G = Gregorian year H = Hijra year.

$$G = H + 626 - \frac{H}{33}$$

$$H = G - 622 + \frac{G - 622}{32}$$

Books for further reading

Islam in General
The Religious Dimension: Islam—Riadh El-Droubie and Edward Hulmes (Longmans 1980)
Islam for Children—Ahmad von Denffer (The Islamic Foundation 1981)
Our Muslim Friends—Anne Farncombe (National Christian Education Council 1977)

History and Heritage
Muhammad and the Arab Empire—John Duckworth (Harrap 1974)
The Rise of Islam—Anton Powell (Longmans 1979)
Mohammed: His Times & Influence—Viola Bailey and Ella Wise (Chambers 1976)
The Buildings of Early Islam—Helen and Richard Leacroft (Hodder & Stoughton 1976)
The Moors—Gerald Hawting (Sampson Low 1978)
Muslim Spain—Duncan Townson (Cambridge University Press 1973)
The Spread of Islam—Michael Rogers (Phaidon 1976)

Muslims in Britain
Understanding your Muslim Neighbour—Muhammed and Maryam Iqbal (Lutterworth Educational 1976)
Nahda's Family—Madeleine Blakely (A & C Black 1977)
Shabnam's Day Out—Joan Solomon (Hamish Hamilton 1980)
Gifts and Almonds—Joan Solomon (Hamish Hamilton 1980)

Islam in the Modern World
Turkey—David Hotham (Macdonald Educational 1975)
Egypt—Michael von Haag (Macdonald Educational 1975)
Saudi Arabia—Eugene Gordon (Oak Tree Press Co. Ltd 1975)
Pakistan—Jon A. Teta (Oak Tree Press Co. Ltd 1972)
The Middle East—Maureen Abdullah (Macdonald Educational 1980)
The Arab World Today—Richard Tames (Kaye & Ward 1980)
The Middle East in the Twentieth Century—Richard I. Lawless (Batsford 1980)
Pakistani Village—Ailsa & Alan Scarsbrook (A & C Black 1979)
Arab Village—Roderic Dutton & John B. Free (A & C Black 1980)
The Oil States—W. B. Fisher (Batsford 1980)
The Muslim Guide—Mustafa Yusuf McDermott (The Islamic Foundation 1980)
Approaches to Islam—Richard Tames (John Murray 1982)

Places to visit

Here is a list of museums and art galleries which have interesting collections of items from the Muslim World. But it is advisable to make enquiries before you go as in some cases the exhibits may be in reserve collections or not normally on public display.

Major collections
Cambridge, Fitzwilliam Museum—
especially carpets, pottery.

Edinburgh, Royal Scottish Museum—
metalwork, armour, pottery and costume.

Glasgow, Burrell Collection, Camphill Museum—
carpets, pottery, metalwork.
Museum and Art Gallery—
weapons.

London, British Museum and King's Library—
comprehensive collection.
Science Museum—
scientific instruments.
Tower of London, New Armouries—
weapons, armour.
Victoria and Albert Museum—
comprehensive collection, notable for carpets.

Manchester Museum—
special collection of bows, weapons, armour.
Museum of the History of Science—
scientific instruments.

Sheffield Art Gallery—
pottery, paintings (Persia and Indian sub-continent).

Smaller collections
Aberdeen, University of Aberdeen Anthropological Museum—
some pottery.

Bath, Victoria Art Gallery—
little, uncatalogued, ceramics and some illuminated pages from manuscripts.

Batley, Bagshaw Museum—
some ceramics mainly of Multan (Pakistan).

Birmingham, City Museum and Art Gallery—
various.

Bradford, City Art Gallery—
uncatalogued collection from Indian subcontinent; available for loan by schools.

Bristol, City Museum and Art Gallery—
various exhibitions.

Cardiff, The Castle—
contains examples of 'Moorish' architecture.

Durham, Gulbenkian Museum of Oriental Art, University of Durham—
various.

Ipswich Museum—
carpets, weapons and domestic items.

London, Horniman Museum—
musical instruments.
The Most Venerable Order of St. John of Jerusalem Museum—
some armour and coins especially from the Holy Land.
National Army Museum—
mostly in store, especially from India.
Wallace Collection—
arms and armour.
Royal Artillery Museum, Rotunda Woolwich—
various weapons and armour.

Maidenhead, The Henry Reitlinger Bequest—
basically ceramic, a 'Persian Room'.

Merseyside County Museums, Departments of Antiquities and Ethnology—
mainly in store, manuscripts, pottery, metalwork, domestic items.

Oxford, Pitt Rivers Museum—
various examples of Muslim craftsmanship and some weapons.

Stoke-on-Trent, City Museum and Art Gallery—
good collection especially of Persian ceramics.

Index

Illustration credits
Key to position of illustrations:
(T) top, (C) centre,
(B) bottom, (R) right,
(L) left.

Artists
Aziz Al-Naib: 35
Nick Farmer: 8-9, 10, 12, 14
Tony Payne: 18, 20-21, 24

Photographic sources
Art and Architecture Collection: 12, 16, 23, 36(B), 37(B)
Dr. Abdul-Haleem: 11
BPC Library/Chester Beatty Library, Dublin: 15(T,B)
BPC Library/Wellcome Institute: 39
Daily Telegraph Colour Library: title page, 19, 24, 25(T)
Sonia Halliday: 36, 37(T)
Robert Harding Picture Library: cover, 14, 18, 28-29, 34(B), 40(R)
Michael Holford: 38(L)
Geoff Howard: 31(T)
Alan Hutchison Library: contents page, 8(T,C), 16(B), 17, 20, 21, 22(T) 29(T), 32, 35, 41(T)
Alan Hutchison Library/ From 'Pilgramage to Mecca' by Mohamed Amin: 25
MEPHA: 38(R)
Rex Features/Sipa Press: 10, 41(B)
Richard Tames: endpapers, 8(B), 22(B), 27, 28(T), 30(L), 40(L)
John Topham Picture Library/Bente Fasmer: 34(T)
John Topham Picture Library/Christine Osborne: 26, 30(R), 31(B), 33T,B)
ZEFA: 13